BELOVED
poems, prose & lyrics

Christa Wells

becoming REAL
Christa Wells

ISBN-13:978-1-7353496-1-9

Cover Photograph by Sofia Wells
Cover Design by Francisco Nogueira

For my children--
Aidan, Sofia, Zachary, Rowan & Samuel
and for the Beloved

CONTENTS

PREFACE

The childhood of my memory is a well-stocked pond of imaginative play with my three siblings; long drives in a blue van across Europe and the United States, often with grandparents and Aunt Linda crammed in; and songs and dances made up and performed in the living room for family and friends. In my mind, Mom is in a continuous dance of hosting, gathering and counseling anyone in need, and Dad moves between throwing the ball with us in the yard and polishing his combat boots at the table.

We relocated frequently, traveled with a cooler full of bread and bologna, camped and swam, climbed trees and followed Dad as he ran, on our bikes, never knowing where we'd finally stop and call Mom for a ride home.

All of these memories, I now understand, are indicative of a rare childhood--rich in love, safety and joy. I credit my parents' great love of God, adventure and community for giving me such a taste of belovedness and freedom.

Even so, when I lost my marriage, and more, after two beautiful decades, I found myself tumbling into a fearful abyss. I was terrified that nothing would be left of me when all was said and done. This book of poems, prose and lyrics tell part of the story of what I found while falling, and rising again.

Christa Wells, 17 Oct 2020

POEMS & PROSE

To Answer Your Question

Yes.
You will die
a few more deaths.

You will stare at the ceiling
of one tomb or another
feel the gushing roaring ache of
absence.

Don't let fear become more than a tightness
at the back of your throat,
a bird in the ribcage,

The first death shaped your hands into keys,
your shoulder blades into wings,
and your heart into a book of poems

that will always remember the way out.
The first death gave you Life.
Do not lay it down.

Bellow

When your body doubles
over and you hear the bellow
of an animal
escape your mouth--
let it come.

Let it moan and rage
pace the wooded
night til day breaks--
if it takes years.

Befriend your agony
as it shudders and stills
and you perceive the sun
scaling the sky across the canyon
of your loss.

72 Degrees

This feels like Costa Rica,
I say, meaning 72 degrees
is all it takes to take me back

eleven weeks of African tulip
trees with one whose love
for me was absolute

and five children whose existence
proved mine. In an instant
all is upon me.

What I mean is: air
is the sole condition
for reliving
what cannot be recalled.

Body and Soul

My body said to my soul:
Please open, please rest, please let go.
My neck is tight, my back aches
my stomach won't take food.

My soul said to my body:
I hear you.
I want so much to do what you ask—
If only you would carry
me to walk among the pines
or listen by the river.
Then I would remember to be alive,
you would forget to suffer,
and together we would dance—

But I cannot get there without you.

The Old Trick

Since age fourteen,
I have loved sleep.

In those solitary years,
I longed for night
to fall and dreams to follow
me into daylight so I could be gone
when I appeared present,
and present in an elsewhere
that was preferable and inside which,
I was preferable.

Thirty years forward I lay still
in bed, alone again.
But the old trick won't take.

There is a light
lining the edges of my closed door,
stealing through blinds
no matter how they are arranged,
and I am awake.

So I succumb to a new dream,
which does not include a better version
of anything or anyone,
but does include the possibility of pain,
the remembrance of resurrection
and the reality of a poem
written by candlelight
moments before dawn.

Songs We Sing

Come here. Let me see you.
I've been listening at the caverned
access to your soul--I have something to say.

First of all, this place is an echo chamber.
Second, only great music should be played
this loudly. This is not great music.

How easy it is to nick the vein
and the old tune come spilling out!

You thought it sealed
but now a credible-sounding voice
runs the halls, screaming:

> fool!
> fool!
> fool!

And you nod your head and tap your foot
while tears roll down your cheeks.

I've come to cup your precious
face and say: This is not the truth about you.

This is a voice you would not in a thousand
years allow near your own child.

Why do you hope someone will fight
for you, when you do not fight for you?

Now then. Wrap your warm body
around your fetus-curled heart,
sing to her this new refrain:

> what a beauty
> what a keeper
> what a dearly-loved creature
> I am
> I am
> I am.

Sing this one at full volume.

Forgiveness

You ask it to settle
over your skin like fleece
when you've only begun
to feel the chill.

Forgiveness, you believe,
wants to believe you when you say
you have risen above, learned
a thing or two, grown stronger,
brave as a baby bird.

You ask for one weightless
moment, just one,
a system hack
to make it come faster
some small relief.

Forgiveness, you hear,
is a declaration,
a measure of generosity
the decision to give up all hope
of having had a better past--
a kindness to self.

First, dear one, ask
to feel the full weight,
to take in what has been taken.
Ask sorrow to swaddle
you one more night.

Life Is

Don't be alarmed by tears
yours or mine--let them come.

Don't be shy about laughter
reach for it--daily!

Don't measure your words
so carefully they lack
the passion love requires.

Life is more than weeping,
more than remembering to be amused,
more than giving language to affection.

But it is never less.

If I Were God

If I were God,
I would have you feel
the lightness of spring
leaves uncurling
and know that you, too,
are a beginning.

I would have you spread
your fingers to catch
the falling light
pour dusk
over your palm
like an open field.

I would lead you like a song
and follow you like a shadow
I would have you never stop
wandering
til your skirts are ragged
and full of gathered gold.

I would set your tender
spirit free
and show you I am
not less but more than you imagined,
that my house is made of laughter
and salvaged parts

If I were God
I would write your name
on ten thousand post-it notes
hang them all
around the world
for you to find

and every witnessed beauty
would be a conversation
between your heart
and mine.

Arrington Vineyards

When you find someone
has left a lantern
waiting in the woods,
consider--
you may not be such a loner
after all.
There are many ways
to keep each other company--
and many ways to be kept
by God.

Most Beautiful

We've grown so close, the Lord and I
that I no longer even glance
in the mirror before we meet.

He has seen me shimmer
pink with pleasure,
seen me shrinking and pale.

Still I haven't been able to talk Him out of love
or into leaving me for someone with blue eyes
or a foreign accent.

He listens like He's never heard this before
like He has all the time in the world
like I am--important.

If his attention towards me sounds improbable
like the fantasy of a lonely woman
I of all people can understand that.

But I've tested him--believe me
nothing has gone unspoken and still
I wake to his heartbeat

his whispers falling
like rosebuds in my hair,
and when everything hurts I know

I am most beautiful
when we are together--yes, even I
can see that.

Breakthrough

When my fist
goes through the glass
don't you worry
don't try to stop me.

These windows
are mine.
It is my body
that lives here.

Sometimes things break
to breathe.
Sometimes panes
become portals.

How to Listen

I am unafraid
of a salted bath
at 10am on a Tuesday
or a slow coffee
at noon. Thoughts
fall from faucets
and rise
from coffee
that may not arrive
on your desk at 9am
sharp. Be courageous
about climbing
down
into the part of your
soul that knows
that God
sometimes sounds
like water.

Unprolific

I shall write my poems
under blankets in winter.

It's still summer.

The grass and the sun
keep climbing
all over me.

Like a River

Sometimes beauty
breaks the soul
from her barricade
and she falls
like a river
to the dirt floor
before running
free.

You are yet to see
how simple the moment
that gives your heart
back into your own hands.

It may be the Bermudagrass
bent blades underfoot
you took for granted
until this morning.

Or the song
that played
just as you pulled
into your driveway
and the rain began.

What Matters Now

What matters now
is a good imagination,
an authentic journey,
and rivers of compassion.

What matters now
is paying attention
and making a meaningful
contribution.

What matters is loving
the world more this morning
than you did last night
and belonging

to at least one person, you,
and to something still greater,
even if you're not sure
what to call it.

What matters here
is your willingness to shake hands
with summer and winter
even if they aren't your favorite

and to throw cold water
on your face on the mornings
when hot dread
fogs the mirror.

What matters most
is that you keep a lemon bright
sphere of trust twirling
in your ribcage
and your body
lifting
 you lifting
  you lifting
   you

I Will Be

Yesterday, on the twelfth
or twenty-first day of rain
there was a brief break

in the clouds.
The sun, forgotten
in the forecast,

threw open the drapes
strolled onto the stage
and just stood there awhile.

See? she said, I am
the boss of me.

I swear she looked straight
at me in the front row—
winked.

I whispered,
I will be exactly
like her when I grow up.

How I Feel About You

When a person
reads like a poem
simple, astonishing, true--
a kindred life telling mine
with a spare line--
when I find myself at home
in the sounds that fall
from a stranger's mouth,

all my spirit
breaks into a gallop.

You are like this--and I can't help
but take out my pencil, underline
my favorite parts.

Crush

I wish I knew
how to be guarded
how to hold a new bloom
without feeling in my limbs
such fretful tension
over every
single
slow-peeling
petal.

I wish I knew
how to love
all seasons equally
like a good parent.
I wish to be
like the unreadable faces.

Instead my skin runs ahead
to tell the whole class
how unreasonably happy,
how needlessly nervous,
how strangely in favor
I am of these balmy nights--

As I have sung,
I have a crush on the whole world.
How to carry on
as if it were not so?

Hold Me, Love

I can't tell you all I've seen
since this morning

when I pledged,
come what may, to keep my eyes wide.

I am over my head
in the great and temporal now

flooded in feelings
no one has named for me

frantic to fly, and to stay,
with you, without you--

how hungry I am, how aching this affection,
peaceful and agitated in turns.

Hold me, Love, in this ephemeral light
so I do not disappear.

What We've Forgotten

It is good to recognize
that you don't need to convince
anyone of anything--
not of what you think Jesus
meant about the eye of the needle
or how to load the dishwasher
or that you are somehow both brilliant
and humble, no, you can simply
load the forks and move on.

It's good to remember
you are free to choose your bathing suit,
your breakfast,
your books and bands
and whether you will dance--
or sit and smile.

Your loved ones are free to scoff
and misunderstand
and you are still free to choose.

It is good to believe
that you don't know what is best
for everybody, you really
do not, perhaps not even for yourself--
which is good cause for becoming
a better listener.

It's good to recall
that you came wailing
and flailing, your first breath
your commission to live
and be what you are.

Can you imagine--
love asking for nothing?
Your young mother,
watching the fall and rise
of your chest, soft smiling
back at you?

Confession

I love us best in crisis.

Traffic lights malfunction
and faceless strangers
co-regulate
flow together.

Tornados tear roofs from homes,
and neighbors who have not grilled together
come together,
feed and rebuild.

A virus cuts through countries
and we are shut in but not out
virtually dependent
on friendship, family.

We become again connected
as we always have been, and re-membered
one family one planet one universe
expanded, expanding, enclosed
gathered in distance
seeing how these bodily borders
might free us from the delusion
of separation.

I love us best in crisis
when we feel
how much we miss
each other.

I Have Not Tasted My Last First

I want to believe
I have not tasted my last first
brambleberry crisp ice cream
or opened the final gift beneath the tree
with my name on it.

I do not judge myself
for this greediness,
this element of aliveness
that also sings me into the woods
to walk until crickets call
to crouch low and wait
watching

for the singular meteorite
of new thought
that will any minute now
pierce the veil
of my understanding
and just like that open the earth
leaving the landscape of my life
forever altered.

I dream of meteorites
as some dream of weekends,
knowing no greater bliss
than a destined disruption
to the perimeter of my possibility.

Weirder

You get weirder
every day
she said in love
and I smiled,
yes,
knowing I am
finding my way back
to the beginning,
our universal nativity
where we appeared
wild divinity
in straw beds
among creatures
too busy being
to mock or criticize—
today that is my aim:
be too busy
being.

Annie's Song

Sometimes God,
finding me weary
of myself and my work
and humanity herself,
pulls me onto the grass
takes up his old guitar
and sings to me

Come let me love you,
I hear.

Slow Waves

There is a way to hover
above the waters
of your circumstances
with compassionate
detachment; a way to wait
with your pen half an inch
over the blank page;
a way to meet your life
like an infinitude
of quarantined mornings
where what is urgent
is also quiet and unhurried.
There is a way to make love
a question of ongoing curiosity,
to give your life to discovering
delight, holding and unfolding
another soul in your mystified gaze,
looking on what is real,
even if you do not understand it,
with the same joyful acceptance
you offer the slow waves
at your ankles.
There is a way to live
without a furrowed brow.
It asks you to ask.
It asks you to play with light.
It asks you to admit your magic.

Blackbird

What you have found you must not lose
What you have seen you cannot unsee
What has been returned to you is yours

What you have learned you will practice
What you have released has released you
What you now hold holds you tenderly

What has seen you is kind
What has hated you was blind
What you have sown now rises to greet you

What grows within is a wordless fortitude
What you have compassion for you do not fear
What surrounds you is a mirror

What you are given is what you ask for
What you sing is singing back to you.

Before Opening My Eyes

Beloved.

My life is open to you,
my heart is open to you,
my palms are open to you.

I receive the strength
I will need for today's work,
the courage to envision new paths,
the bounding joy of aliveness,

and the peace of a soul
whose face has never stopped
being kissed.

Wayfinding

Dear one, it's time. Mark the miles with an altar of thanksgiving.
Part tenderly with the past. What brought you here will not carry
you on.

Another way awaits your awakening. Now is the time to envision
what you cannot know, what you have never been shown. Over
the edge, beyond the final outposts.

You cannot conjure it; you can only wonder. You can only grin at
the idea of a foreign city rising up within you that emboldens everything without. You can only decide, eventually, that freedom
is unfathomably possible.

Remember, beloved, that just because you cannot see a road out
doesn't mean there isn't one. It only means you can't see it from
here. It may not appear as a road at all. A river, a sky, a winding
staircase, a dragon's wings. Have your eyes open; expect to be
surprised.

Some people won't understand. People for whom
you care deeply and with whom you have lived closely will nod
and steer the talk to neighborhood gossip or the virtues of staying
close to home.

It's okay. A person can love you and not understand.
A person can love you and still not approve. Approval is not
what is needed. Waiting for it could be fatal to what you have
come to be and accomplish.

Already, people you held close have let you go.
You also let you go.

Now you are reclaiming yourself--do not make the same mistakes again. You must not, now that you know better.

You have confused people for Source when they were always channels of love. People have disappointed you, but Love cannot. Love will not. Love has witnessed and supported every breath of your dear life. Your beating heart is all the evidence you need.

Your soul hasn't always understood Love, but Love has always understood you.

There will be a day when you look over your shoulder and see it clearly. Clear as a blue sky in May--how much has taken place and how you are not the same. How you were stuck in rumination and scarcity, nostalgia and fear, certain you would not laugh again.

You were right to think it would take a miracle. You were right to believe it could not come quickly.

Still.

There is a day coming when you will realize you are somewhere new and that you yourself are undeniably new.

Bow and bend your body to the light until one day joy erupts small and green, a promise yet curled, to be watched with expectancy.

My love, this is a season of unburying. Get your hands dirty.

See. Love. Laugh. Learn from everyone, especially the children and joyful elders. Especially the daughter who reminds you that the essential ingredients of a good life are: a portable dance floor, a movie projector, roller skates, joyful friends, and good cheese.

Allow for the possibility that there is a way of Life you have yet to meet. Pioneer the wondrous and tragic terrain of your experience.

Lift your eyes to perceive something Entirely Other waiting for you.

Aliveness.

The deepest desire of the human creature, though we name it differently and run from it relentlessly.

We meet Aliveness on the courageous path. You find it by embracing your uncertainty. Dear one, your love of mystery is your act of faith.

Take a slow step into the unknown. Allow the old life to come to an end.

This is your beginning.

VELVETEEN
lyrics

Down Down Low

Sometimes you gotta go dark
Sometimes you gotta be quiet
Sometimes you gotta get far from
The voices that stir up violence
Everybody wants to talk
Nobody wants to listen
Everybody wants to talk
Nobody wants to listen

You gotta get get get
Down down low
You gotta turn turn turn it
Down down low
You gotta take it take it take it
Down down low
You gotta get down low

Sometimes you gotta go first
Sometimes you gotta be sorry
Sometimes you're gonna get hurt and
Go back to where you started
Everybody wants to win
Nobody wants to listen
Everybody wants to win
Nobody wants to listen

Find the voice that speaks in every tongue
Hear the song that writes a thousand more
If we listen well before it's said and done
There'll be harmony we've never heard before

Hear the whisper of humility
Love will write a sweeter melody

Come After Me

I was 17, running through the back woods
Sat down by the river with my book
It felt so good
Getting lost in my thoughts
Dreaming about being found
Could anybody hear my heart say

Come after me, come after me, come after me
I want to be, I want to be, I want to be
Worth the grand pursuit
Wanted by you
So if I go, I need to know
Your love will come after me

Used to feel you thinking of me from across town
Hard for me to reach you
When you stand across the room now
So I'm climbing the hills
Just to get to your heart
'Cause I keep hoping that I'll see you

Though I want you, I know I'll be okay
If you leave, I'll keep walking anyway
Find me in the forest
Where the riverbed sings
Tell me you've been looking
You've been looking for me

Hold This House Up

I wasn't awake to notice the rain
I wasn't awake
Until I saw you kneeling in the mud
I added the cost, I gathered the rope
I sounded the bell, but oh
The damage had already been done

I know it's late - I know it's late
But I think it's not too late
To get our hands dirty
And act like it's worth being saved

Will you help me hold this house up
Will you help me hold this house up
Will you help me hold this house up
And let the waters pass beneath

You want to let go, let it go on
You haven't the heart
For one more disappointing turn of events
But look at the stone under our feet
Still in its place
And I think that these old bones could stand a chance

I know it's hard - I know it's hard
But I think it's not too hard
To fix it together, maybe stronger than ever before

Butterfly

I know you know it now
You've got it figured out
I'm only human
I'm only human after all

Answers were easier then
I'd little chance of being wrong
These days are different and
I'm only human after all

We don't have to see eye to eye
You will always be a friend of mine

So go where you must go
Be who you need to be
I'll meet you on the road
Tell me what you see
Butterfly, my butterfly

I would be lying to
Pretend I want to lose
Having you with me
I want you with me, yes, I do

But if I know anything
It's there's always beauty yet to come
So I'll let you go since
I know you're coming back, my love

And I'll be waiting with bated breath
To hear you laughing close again

Oh, now the time has come and I am not afraid
To see your wings unfold
Against the brightness of the sun
And you will soar
You will soar

So be who you need to be
I'll meet you on the road
You can tell me what you see
Go where you must go
Be who you need to be
Show me what you make
Of all of your good dreams
Butterfly, my butterfly

One Day

It's hard to sing when you're crying
Hard to leave when you're tied down
It's hard to sleep when you're fighting
For your life like you are right now
There's only so much more you can stomach
Though it's more than you thought
And you only keep moving
By the grace of God

You're doing one day
One breath
One prayer
One thing at a time
One word
One step
One hope
In a coming light
Don't try to swallow the ocean
Keep doing one day
Til one day you're free

You could escape in a daydream
But you'd wind up right back here
Up to your waist in the maybes
No use hiding on the back stairs
Hear the peculiar voice in the forest
Calling open the doors
It'll take a few battles
To win this war

Oh, I see you laughing
On the other side
Where the walls have tumbled
And the flowers grow wild
Oh, I see you laughing
On the other side
With your broken heart
Under open sky

Holy Ground

You think singers & dreamers
Invent escape from the real
Oh, but they have eyes to see
What must be revealed
There's a kingdom before us
Whose gate is always open
Looks like earth & sounds like human voices
And it feels like heaven

Holy, Holy
All that is within us
All that is without
All of life is holy ground

If your compass is pointing to wealth & fame
It has been altered
There is only one true north
One good road to follow
When you lift your eyes you'll find
The view is ever wider
'Til the vanities fade and your love burns
Brighter and brighter

We'll take our shoes off
Honor the moments of our days
Find our treasure
When we give our love away
What a gift to hold this in our hands
Behold the beauty
See the face of God in a grain of sand

Velveteen

Love spoke my name
I felt life run through me
Reborn in the flames
Nothing can undo me
Ooh, I believe
That I'm becoming

So if my beauty starts to fade
Well, I've been held in a thousand ways
If my heart looks broken in
Then I've been brave enough to live
If perfect turns to perfect mess
And all your love is all that's left
Then I'm as real as real can be
Call me Velveteen

Shadow and light
I learned to let them find me
Coming alive
Feels a lot like dying
Ooh, I believe
That I'm becoming

I know it's true no matter
True no matter how I feel
'Cause I'm becoming
I'm becoming real

PACIFIC
lyrics

I Can Do Better

I let my hair down
You showed me all over town
But every flower you gave me
Has dropped its petals to the ground
And lately I pray

Don't let me love what will not love me back
I think I'm done with that

'Cause I waited for you to be what you can't be
I let you hold me, but you can't have me
I thought that you would be a shelter
But I can do better

Sweet Sadness, my old friend
How good it was to sit with you again
But you have no heart to save me
And I've got so much left to live
So lately I pray

Don't let me love what will not love me back
I think I'm done with that

I've got a love that loves me right
My lover makes me come alive
There's nothing like it
There's nothing like it

Let It Out

I'm looking up at the stars
From the bottom of a well
Feels like we might be rising
But it sure is cold down here

I'm looking over the earth
From the inside of a cloud
That refuses to rain or dissipate
It seems I've forgotten how to

Let it out, let it out, let it out, let it out

So I'm gonna walk in the forest
Deep in the silent green
'Til I get to the place where I know it's safe
And I'll fall down on my knees and

Let it out, let it out, let it out, let it out

Sometimes it's only
Only beauty
That breaks us open
You don't see it coming
'Til you are weeping
Like a child again

Look at the stars coming closer
I taste the tears on my lips
Look at the stars coming closer
I taste the tears on my lips now

Falling Up

I built a house of my beliefs
That house has really been good to me
But I'm less impressed than I used to be
I started out following the trail
It took me to the coast and my heart set sail
He knew I would find my way here

I came to meet my love, came to meet my love
I came to meet my love, came to meet my love
And it feels like I'm falling up, I'm falling up
Into love, love, love, love

We walk together under open sky
We talk and dream late into the night
It's easy to believe my eyes
I wanna set a table out on the sea
For all the souls afraid of being free
The light is different out here

Oh, he's leaving me love notes, leaving me love notes
We're taking the backroads, taking the backroads
He's keeping me so close, and Lord knows what I don't
So don't worry 'bout me, don't worry 'bout me

I came to meet my love, came to meet my love

Pacific

You are not too much
You are not underwhelming
You are not a number
Or a contestant for my love

You are not your past
You are not a victim
You are not what you were told
You are not who you were back then
You are not who you were back then

You're the Pacific under white lights
You're my favorite kind of stormy night
And I'm always ready for the deep dive
I'd go walk in the rain with you anytime

You are not your thoughts
You are not your emotions
You are not too far to be found
You are not beyond knowing
You are not beyond knowing

And when the days are short
And your heart is longing
Don't go hiding away
Lay your head down on me
Nowhere else I wanna be

Meet Me At The Water

Tossing after midnight
Playing back the day, kicking myself
How is it that moonlight
Turns my better thoughts into something else
Easy in the morning, for me
When I open my eyes
But in the dark I hear some pretty good lies

Meet me at the water
When the sun goes down
When the sun goes down
When the sun goes down
We'll stay up together
Learn to laugh at ourselves
Laugh at ourselves
We'll laugh at ourselves

We'll find it funny
After some talk and a good cry
Broken hearts, no money
Let the fire burn til we're good and tired
Drink to all the true things we've seen
Tell our stories of love
How it stays when the rest is gone

You bring the chocolate
and I'll bring the cheap wine
Open your heart, I'll open mine
We'll lose sleep just to be alive

Western Shoreline

I flew out to Palo Alto
From Nashville in mid-July
I felt the sea salt burning in my lungs
So keenly I could cry
'Cause I love my little front porch
And waking up in my own bed
But I'd been home for a while
I was getting lost inside my head

I drove up to Monte Bello
For a solitary climb
But I met a man who knew the trails
We walked the last few miles
He told me we were standing
On the San Andreas Fault
And if it opened we'd both be goners
Within a minute, ready or not

Well, I'm not afraid of dying
But I'm dead set on being alive
Give me something to stop my heartbeat
Like the western shoreline

I looked over the Pacific
From the height of Mussel Rock
And I saw the waves come rolling
With the current of my thoughts
Four decades I was breathing
Without filling up my lungs
Now I'm headed for the edge
I'm running right into the sun

Ready to Go

I'm starting over
I see the sun rising up ahead
I have let the past fall from my shoulders
I'm throwing open the suitcase on my bed

And there's no room for what you never gave me
There's no room for what I gave away
I'll take a heart that's stronger for the breaking
I'll wear a smile 'cause I'm not waiting another day

I'm ready to go
I'm ready to go
I'm ready to go

Fear kept me holding
Onto a life that was not holding me
'Til I woke and found my love unfolding
Just like a blanket, she wrapped herself around me

And I know that goodbyes are never easy
But I think we should say them anyway
I want to thank you for the pain I'm leaving
It took me deeper, sent me out and on my way

Oh, I'm taking roads I'd never have chosen
I'm turning the stones I'd never have noticed
I feel the universe conspiring for my good
And I'm ready to go

GRATITUDE

My heart is full. My ability to create anything at all is due to the fact of the generous love and support I've received from others. The great gift of having such champions is not lost on me.

In particular, I owe gratitude to my parents for encouraging my imagination from the start and for saving me in all sorts of ways following my divorce. To those who've joined together to fund my albums--and my beloved Patrons who support my work monthly--you are way-makers, my friends. Nothing moves from mind to material without you. Grateful to Emily Hines and Emily Dempsey who helped me get this thing going and bring it to fruition. Friends and listeners who have encouraged me to return to poetry--something I set aside years ago--THANK YOU for giving it back to me.

Lastly to the many poets, authors and songwriters who have inspired and accompanied me on this way of words... I stand humbly on your shoulders to see the way.

Christa Wells is an American singer and songwriter who began practicing the art of beginning again as a child, experiencing frequent relocations as the daughter of an army officer. Writing about growth and the grief that often accompanies it has been a centerpoint of her work, as well as mentoring others in the invaluable skill of living a life of wonder and creating beauty from heartache. An award-winning songwriter, she has collaborated with and written for a number of other performing artists and released eight albums of original music independently. She has five children and currently lives in Nashville, Tennessee. This is her first book of poems.

Christa Wells on Spotify